BLACKBIRDS IN SEPTEMBER

BLACKBIRDS IN SEPTEMBER

SELECTED SHORTER POEMS OF

JÜRGEN BECKER

TRANSLATED BY

OKLA ELLIOTT

BLACK LAWRENCE PRESS

Executive Editor: Diane Goettel

Book design: David Bowen

ISBN: 978-1-62557-938-6

First edition: December 2015

Printed in the United States of America

0 9 8 7 6 5 4 3 2 1

CONTENTS

ACKNOWLEDGMENTS

Many thanks to the editors and magazines that first published several of the translations in this collection:

Absinthe: "Amsterdam"; "Belgian Coast"; "Daytime, a Connection"

The Adirondack Review: "The Year 1932"; "Village Outskirts with Gas Station / 1"; "Village Outskirts with Gas Station / 2"

Arch Literary Journal: "Once Again"

Black Market Review: "West-East"; "Otherwise Nobody"; "Altenbeken"

ĕm: "Hell, Sartre Said, Is Other People"

Indiana Review: "Oderbruch"

International Poetry Review: "An Almost Forgotten Thing"

InTranslation: "A Worn-out Machine"; "Dublin in Bloomtime"; "The Window at the End of the Corridor"

Life and Legends: "Old Film"; "Tell Me How You're Doing"

The Literary Review: "On Mouse's Way; Street Construction"; "Paris"

The Los Angeles Review: "Sun or Moon"

The McNeese Review: "Two Women"; "Near Andy Warhol"; "Sunday Evening"; "Zoo District"

Natural Bridge: "Correspondent"

Per Contra: "Autumn Story"; "Chronicle"; "Renaissance";
"Possibilities for Paintings"

Plume: "A Provisional Topography"; "Sooner or Later"; "One
of the Many Stories of Sounds"

Prairie Schooner: "In the Wind"; "Correspondent";
"Oderbruch"; "Autumn Story"; "A Provisional Topography";
"Poem about Snow in April"

A Public Space: "A Foreign Affair"; "In the Wind"

In addition to the editors of the above journals, I need to thank
many people. First and foremost, allow me to thank Jürgen
Becker for his amazing work and his willingness to entrust it to
me. Thanks to Diane Goettel, Daniele Pantano, and everyone at
Black Lawrence Press for bringing the book into existence and
believing in it. David Bowen has been, per usual, a pleasure
to work with; his design skills and his patience with my many
requests proved phenomenal. I would also like to thank Dick
Davis and Andrew Hudgins for their encouragement during
the early phases of my work with Becker's poetry. Big thanks
to Sanna Stegmaier for proofreading the German and double-
checking my translation. And, looking further back, I would
like to thank the study abroad program at UNC-Greensboro
for providing me a scholarship to support my year abroad
in Germany without which I never would have learned the
language or been exposed to Becker's work. Finally, a huge
thank-you to my sisters Flora and Vickie who have supported
me in everything — *ohne euch, nichts.*

TRANSLATOR'S PREFACE

Umberto Eco calls translation the art of failure, and I have failed variously in my attempts to render Jürgen Becker's poetry into English — though Samuel Beckett's dictum that one must try again and fail better comes immediately to mind as a counterpoint to Eco's observation about the impossible task of translation. Over the past decade, I have followed Beckett's advice, trying again and again to get at the spirit of Becker's poetry, failing again and again, but, I hope, failing better along the way.

I first discovered Jürgen Becker's work during a year-long study abroad in Germany while I was an undergraduate. When I returned to the United States, I continued to read his work with ever-increasing interest and began translating his work during graduate school at Ohio State University. Comparative literature scholar and critical theorist Gayatri Spivak has claimed that the best way to read a writer's work is to translate it, and this is perhaps most true in the case of poetry. Once I began translating Becker's poems, I had to find my way into the shape and feel of his lyric idiom in order to recreate it as accurately and effectively as possible in English. Translating his work forced me not only to *read it* with greater care but forced me to *write it* as I constructed the English versions of his poems. That comingling of my language and his makes my relationship to Becker's work unlike any other I have with an author.

What is immediately striking about Becker's work is his ability to track the oddities of consciousness, as well as the unexpected ways he makes ideas and images ricochet off each another. He also renders historically charged content in aesthetically nuanced language masterfully. Becker's work often deals with his childhood experience of the Second World War and the political consequences of the postwar division of Germany. It is perhaps his deft lyric melding of the personal and the historical/political that makes him a truly great poet.

Becker's work fits well in several disciplines, ranging from creative writing to various scholarly fields. For the former, it is often productive to engage with different literary traditions in order to enrich our own. We simply have to remember all that English-language literature has learned from other languages — sonnets from Italian, couplets from French, and, some argue, free verse from Chinese — to realize how true this is. And as for the latter, the fields of memory studies, trauma studies, and European literary studies in general could benefit from further investigation into Becker's work. I hope *Blackbirds in September* proves to be an entry point into a wider consideration of Becker's excellent and far-ranging output.

Finally, a quick note on the structure of the book: I have elected to organize the poems aesthetically as opposed to chronologically. I have, however, listed the poems included here by their German titles and the collections in which they initially appeared in the appendix. There is also the occasional footnote throughout the body of the text when I thought the cultural reference would be lost on an English-language reader, though I have made every effort to keep these to a minimum. I therefore hope to have created the maximum aesthetic pleasure in reading the poems while still offering a critical apparatus that will prove useful for further research.

May the reader enjoy reading these translations as much as I have enjoyed producing them.

— **Okla Elliott**

Im Wind

Amseln, dann andere Stimmen. Es hört nicht auf
im Schnee, wenn mit dem Schnee
eine Neuigkeit kommt, die heute morgen
ganz *wesentlich* ist. Oder wie
siehst du das? Ich sehe den Birnbaum und wie er
(der Birnbaum) reagiert auf den Wind (auf den
Wind). Heute morgen, noch einmal, fiel
die Entscheidung. Krieg
zwischen Elstern und Krähen, nur dieser Krieg,
kein Drumherum, nur diese deutliche Verständigung.
Noch eine Stimme, der nächste Kommentar; es geht
ja (noch einmal) ums Ganze. Stehst du
im Garten? Dann weißt du, tuck tuck, die Amsel hat
zuallererst gewarnt, du weißt es, ich sage es noch
einmal, im Krieg, im neuen Schnee, im Wind.

In the Wind

Blackbirds, then other voices. It doesn't stop
when it snows, when with the snow
a newness comes that is
entirely *essential* this morning. Or how
do you see it? I see the pear tree and how it
(the pear tree) reacts to the wind (to the
wind). This morning, yet again,
the decision fell. War
between magpies and crows, only this war,
no trappings, only this clear understanding.
Yet another voice, the next commentator; it's all about
(yet again) the whole. Are you standing
in the garden? Then you know, tsk tsk, the blackbird
warned above all else, you know, I'll say it yet
again, in war, in the new snow, in the wind.

GEDICHT ÜBER SCHNEE IM APRIL

April-Schnee; schnell; noch einmal
ist fünfzehn Minuten
Winter und völliges Verschwinden
der Krokus-Gebiete
         und
fünfzehn Minuten, in Zukunft,
sagt Warhol, ist Ruhm. Schnell,
ein Gedicht über Schnee im April,
denn schnell ist weg
Stimmung und Schnee
         und plötzlich,
metaphorisch gesagt,
ist Schnee-Herrschaft verschwunden
im Krokusgebiet
und die Regierung des Frühlings regiert.
Nun Frühlings-Gedicht.
Und schnell. Winter ist morgen, wieder,
und neue Herrschaft,
         nein,
nicht morgen: in fünfzehn Minuten,
mit Schnee, wie schnelles Leben,
sagt Warhol, metaphorisch gesagt,
wie Schnee, Verschwinden, April.

POEM ABOUT SNOW IN APRIL

April-snow; quickly; once again
fifteen minutes
of winter and full disappearance
of crocus-regions
                    and
fifteen minutes, in the future,
says Warhol, is fame. Quickly,
a poem about snow in April,
for mood and snow
are quickly gone
                    and suddenly,
metaphorically speaking,
snow-mastery disappeared
in the region of the crocus,
and the regime of spring rules.
So, a spring-poem.
And quickly. Tomorrow it's winter, again,
and new mastery,
                    no,
not tomorrow: in fifteen minutes
with snow, like quick life,
says Warhol, metaphorically speaking,
like snow, disappearing, April.

EINST, IM FEBRUAR

See-Wetter; aber die See nicht.
Diese Erinnerung an Küsten; Küsten
des Exils, die ich so nannte,
einst, als ich hierblieb.

ONCE, IN FEBRUARY

Ocean weather; but not the ocean.
This memory of coasts; coasts
of exile, as I called them
once, when I stayed here.

BELGISCHE KÜSTE

Toccata und Tango; der Nachmittag
nicht hell. Ein Hotel
nach dem andern verwittert;
Ansichtskarten der Emigranten.
Türen, Türen
verweht der Sand, verschwinden
hinter dem Sand. Ruhe der Angler.
Unsichtbares England; Nachrichten
der englischen Sender, im Krieg.
Kinder rennen
mit Bällen, Rädern, Propellern;
Fallschirmjäger da.

BELGIAN COAST

Toccata and tango; the afternoon
not bright. One hotel
weathered after another;
postcards of emigrants.
Doors, doors
are blown away by the sand,
disappear behind the sand. The calm
of anglers. Invisible England; reports
from the British transmitter, wartime.
Children run
with balls, wheels, propellers;
and paratroopers all about.

EINE VORLÄUFIGE TOPOGRAPHIE

An der Weichsel, vor dem Kriege. Nun siehst du
genau, wo wir
hätten weitergehen können, auf dem Weg
übern Damm, der das Nichts des Flußsilbers
trennte von Dingen, die nichts als Schatten
bildeten im Wechsel des Lichts.

Die unbewegte Architektur der Wolken: es ist
dieser Augenblick, der über Jahrzehnte sich hinzieht
und angenommen hat die Farbe von Zeitungspapier.

In der Ferne im Dunkeln zwei Häuser.
Obwohl es ganz hell ist.

Ob Seelen hier wandern . . . jedenfalls, fern
auf dem Damm, sind unterwegs zwei Menschen,
die sich abheben vom Horizont, mitten
in dieser Vergangenheit.

Aber die Baumreihen setzen sich fort, bis
sie verschwinden in einer Linie, die zurückkehrt
auf der anderen Seite des Flusses.

Die Frage, ob so oder ähnlich Konflikte anfingen.

Bei Nacht, und nicht nur nachts, im Konjunktiv.

. . . als käme einem die Böschung entgegen. Dann
ist es klar, daß du nichts steuern kannst
an der Geschichte. Ein Weitergehen, allenfalls
eine ganze private Bewegung, die unentschieden bleibt
zwischen Heimkehr und lingerer Abwesenheit. Diese Jahre,
sagt man, haben Spuren der Bitterkeit hinterlassen.

A PROVISIONAL TOPOGRAPHY

On the Weichsel River, before the war. Now you see
exactly where we
could have gone farther on the path
above the dam separating the Nothing of river-silver
from those things that formed only shadows
in the changing light.

The unmoved architecture of clouds: it is
this moment that over decades has dragged itself
and has adopted the color of newsprint.

In the distance, in the dark, two houses.
Although it's bright as day.

Whether souls wander here . . . in any case, distant,
on the dam, two people walking
stand out against the horizon, in the middle
of this past.

But the rows of trees continue until
they disappear in a line that returns
on the other side of the river.

The question, whether such or similar conflicts began.

At night, and not just nights, in the subjunctive.

. . . as though the embankment were to come against us.
Then it's clear that you can't steer anything in history.
A progression, an altogether private movement stays
undecided between the return home and a further absence.
These years, it's said, have left traces of bitterness.

Aber die Landschaft ist ziemlich still.
Unsichtbar bleibt die Zerstörung, falls es
Zerstörung gibt.

Und vorbei ist die Zeit, die
die folgende, die folgende Zeit hervorgebracht hat.

Nur erzählst du vom Jetzt nichts.

Wahrscheinlich im Sommer. Zu jeder Jahreszeit
erinnert man sich. Zaunpfähle folgen den Pfaden,
oder umgekehrt, überall zugehörig
der Landschaft . . . wem gehört sie? Die Landschaft
setzt Landschaften fort, die sichtbaren bis
zu den unsichtbaren, die auf uns warten.

Eine vorläufige Topographie.
Du kannst sie verwischen. Du kannst sie
Verändern, bis eine Serie entsteht, bis wir erreichen
die Ufer der Wiederholung.

But the landscape is rather quiet.
Invisible the destruction, if in fact
there is destruction.

And the time is passed
which the subsequent, the subsequent time produced.

But you never speak of Now.

Probably in the summer. At that time of year
we remember. Fence posts follow the paths,
or turned around, all of it belonging
to the landscape . . . who owns it? The landscape
leads into landscapes, from the visible ones
to the invisible ones which await us.

A provisional topography.
You can cover it up. You can change
it, until a series emerges, until we achieve
the shore of repetition.

BEZIRK TIERGARTEN

Der Wind hat aufgehört; aufgehört hat
das Geräusch der Machinenpistole; ruhig
steht wieder der Park; ruhig wieder
liegt das Wasser im Kanal.

Zoo District

The wind has stopped; the sound of the machine
pistol has stopped; the park stands quiet
again; quiet again
lies the water in the canal.

ALTENBEKEN

Irgendwo verläuft hier die Grenze,
Truppen werden verladen, Tieflieger,
aber es gibt
keine Tieflieger, Truppen, Grenze,
nur Reisende, Anschlüsse
nach Braunschweig, Köln, Walkenried,
schwarze Bahnsteige
in der Hitze und Leere des Samstags,
eine Reihe von Pappeln
über diesem alten Bahngelände,
das ich erwähnen werde, wenn
ich dir wieder erzähle vom Krieg.

ALTENBEKEN[1]

Somewhere here runs the border
troops are loaded up, low-flying planes,
but there aren't any
planes or troops, no border,
only travelers, connections
for Braunschweig, Cologne, Walkenried,
black train-platforms
in the heat and emptiness of Saturday,
a row of poplars
over this old sprawling station
which I will mention
the next time I tell you about the war.

---

1   A municipality in the district of Paderborn, in North Rhine-West-
phalia, Germany.

Sonst Niemand

halb fünf im grünen Licht
hinter den Stadtwäldern
rollt das erste Gewitter im Jahr weg
eine Reise nach Zürich hat sich entfernt
Mäntel schaukeln in der Garderobe
weiter kreischende Vögel
der Regen kommt noch einmal vorbei

Otherwise Nobody

half past four in the green light
behind the city forests
the first storm of the year rolls away
a journey to Zürich is distancing
coats swing in the closet
further screeching birds
the rain comes one more time

HERBSTGESCHICHTE

Eine Zeichnung, oder auch nur Gekritzel . . . ich hatte
versucht, dem alten, sich senkenden Birnbaum
einen Halt zu geben. Aber die Stütze aus
Bleistiftstrichen mißlang. Nun regiert hier, seit
ein paar Tagen, der Nebel, der es heute
fertiggebracht hat, daß man gar nichts mehr
sieht. So geht das all dieses Jahr,
Strukturen, Fröste, Eulenflug, Kriege im September.

Autumn Story

A sketch, or just some scribbling . . . I had tried
to give the old, sunken pear tree fortification.
But the support of pencil-marks failed. Now,
for a few days already, a fog reigns, one that finally
has finished the job. There's nothing more to see here.
That's how everything has gone this year:
structures, frosts, the flight of owls, wars in September.

CHRONIK

Der Himmel heute ist klar. Ein Wetter für
Bomberpiloten. Gleich brechen sie auf, oder erst morgen,
die Blüten des Rhododendron.

Die Wiesen sind trocken. Am Wiesenrand
stehen Männer und schauen hoch in die Luft, in der
sich der Bussard kreisend entfernt.

Dann macht sie das Fenster zu, die älter
werdende Frau, der unten im Hof der Geländewagen
gehört, mit Seekarten auf dem Beifahrsitz.

CHRONICLE

The sky is clear today. A weather
for bomber pilots. They break open now, or early tomorrow,
the blooms of the rhododendron.

The fields are dry. At the field's edge,
men stand and look high into the air
where the buzzard flies in distancing circles.

Then she closes the window, the aging
woman, who owns the Jeep below, in the courtyard,
the one with a sea chart in the passenger seat.

VIER ZEILEN

Unter Pappeln sitzend, und wieder die Stimme
im Selbstgespräch, das nicht aufhört, bis
alles zermürbt ist; der Wind erleichtert nichts,
der einfach durch die Blätter geht.

Four Lines

Sitting under the poplars, and once again the voice —
talking to itself — it won't stop, until everything
is worn away; the wind doesn't make things easier;
it just blows through the leaves.

AMSTERDAM

Vielleicht Amsterdam, aber der Nebel
ließ nichts zu, keinen Namen
und Ort; das Wasser, die Küsten
verschwunden; wäre tödlich gewesen
eine Bewegung; still saß ich im Bett,
das durch die weißen Räume trieb.

AMSTERDAM

Perhaps Amsterdam, but the fog
obscured everything, erased name
and place; the water, the coasts
vanished; any movement
would have been deadly; I sat
quietly in bed
drifting through the white rooms.

Vormittag, Zusammenhang

sieh mal, der gute Kater liegt jetzt
in der Sonne,
          schlafend, unweit
des Vogels, den er heut morgen
erschlug,
          und deine Bluse
hat jetzt einen Riß.

Daytime, a Connection

take a look, the pleasant tomcat
in the sun now,
            sleeping, not far
from the bird he struck down
this morning,
            and now your blouse
has a rip in it.

WEST-OST

. . . ein Bild mit zwei Köpfen, Stadtsilhouette; vielleicht
Erinnerungen ans Exil. Unterwegs sein nach
Solingen; die nächste Serpentine im Zusammenhang
so vieler Vernissagen. Der Winter kam nicht
an, schwache Rezensenten, wenig Bedeutung vom
kahlen Ast. Andere Spuren führen in
die offene Steppe; abmontierte Eisenbahnschienen
Liegen da, verhängt von Fetzen gefroren Atems;
Gerüchtweise Steckrüben; Gardinen sind nicht
zu haben. Noch einige Muster; Entwürfe
für ein Danach, das nicht mehr stattfand; hier
taucht für eine Weile die Stadtgeschichte
unter; gelegentlich Anfragen, man war
nicht immer da. Dann kreist ein
Marienkäfer überm Papier, zwei, drei Runden,
bis er herabfällt auf die Mark Brandenburg; so rasch
geht die Kälte nicht aus dem Zimmer. . .

WEST-EAST

. . . a picture with two heads, a city skyline; perhaps
memories of exile. To be on the way
to Solingen; the next snaking road in connection
with so many vernissages. Winter didn't arrive,
weak reviewers, little meaning
in the bare branching. Other trails lead
onto the open steppe; dismantled train rails
lie there, covered by the shreds of frozen breath;
Swede-turnip rumors; curtains aren't
to be found. Just a few more patterns; suggestions
for an After This, which no longer existed; here
the city's history is submerged for a while;
occasionally inquiries, we weren't
always there. Then a ladybird circles
above the paper — two, three rounds
until she falls upon Brandenburg's center; the cold
doesn't leave the room so quickly. . .

NOCHMALS

Vorbereitungen für das, was sich hinzieht und hinzieht
bis zu einem Start, der ganz lautlos erfolgen wird.

Niemand merkt was. Es macht eben kein
Geräusch, wenn Spuren entstehen auf einem Feld
der unsichtbaren Entwürfe.

Zuviel schon verraten. Sofort und später
eine ewige Sucherei, und meistens wird etwas
entdeckt, das Falsche.

Falls Zweifel erlaubt sind. Oder ein Apparat
mit Gedächtnis.

Längst hat es aufgehört, und es hat sich
das Gras aufgerichtet bis abends.

Once Again

Preparations for what drags and drags itself
to a start, a thing soundlessly effected.

No one notices it. There's not even
a noise, when tracks show up in a field
of invisible blueprints.

Too much already betrayed. Immediately and later
an eternal searching, and mostly
what's found: the false.

In case doubt is allowed. Or an apparatus
with memory.

It stopped long ago, and the grass,
it stands upright until evening.

ZWEI FRAUEN

1

im Haus der Pfarrerfrau das Telefon
blieb still, und sie wußte auch nie was
von den Festivals unten in der Hafengegend;
am Rand des Haferfeldes stand sie
und hielt sich das Kleid fest

2

noch näher ans Fenster rückt
der Holunder; bis die Suppe kalt ist,
hat sich die Großmutter zweimal bekreuzigt,
weil ich hab nach der Hexe gefragt,
die mit dem Blasrohr, sechzehn und schwarz

Two Women

1

in the house of the vicar's wife, the telephone
was quiet, and she never knew anything
about the festivals down by the harbor;
on the edge of a field of oats she stood
and held her dress tightly to her

2

moving even nearer to the window
the elder; until the soup is cold,
the grandmother crosses herself twice
because I have asked about the witch,
who with the blow-gun, sixteen and black

SONNE ODER MOND

Die Vorwahlnummer von Leipzig. Du zeigst mir
den kleinen Computer, der alles schon weiß, bevor
hinter den Hügeln die Sonne hochkommt. Nur
kennt er die Wörter nicht, die dein Satzgestöber

hinterläßt. Lupinen, wo kamen sie
zuallererst vor? Von vor fünf Jahren
das Telefonbuch, das kannst du vergessen, oder
geht es schon wieder um eine Identität, die nur
mit Akten, Postleitzahlen korrespondiert? Spätestens

morgen die dritte Frage, falls Einer wissen
will, ob hinter den Hügeln nicht möglicherweise
der Mond stand. Der Mond, auf den immer Verlaß
ist, auch wenn es Zweifel gibt an der Neutralität
seiner Strahlen. Wofür ich mich entscheide,

ich wollte jetzt telefonieren. Nur
mußte ich wieder warten, so oft ich Zahlen,
Buchstaben tippte, stündlich nach den Nachrichten.

SUN OR MOON

The Leipzig area code. You show me
the small computer that already knows everything
before the sun rises behind the hills. It's only that
it doesn't know the words your flurry of sentences

leaves behind. Lupins, where did they come from
originally? From five years ago,
the telephone book, you can just forget that—or
is it once again about an identity, which only corresponds
with records, zip codes? At the latest

tomorrow morning, the third question, in case one wants
to know, whether the moon was behind the hills.
The ever-reliable moon, even when there is doubt
about the neutrality of its gleam. For which I'm in favor;

I wanted just now to make a phone call. It's only that
I had to wait again; so often have I typed numbers,
letters, every hour after the news.

SONNTAGABEND

Die Milch in der roten Kanne kommt
direkt aus dem Kuhstall. Ein dunkler Weg,
abends gegen sechs, und nur der Himmel
über Leverkusen ist hell. Die beiden Alten:
mein Jahrgang; während ich unterwegs war
in anderen Städten, versorgten sie ihren Hof.
Der ist der letzte, und die Jungens bauen
über den Ställen Wohnungen aus. Roststellen,
Beulen; brauchen wir die neue Kanne?

Sunday Evening

The milk in the red canister comes
direct from the cow stall. A dark path,
around six in the evening, and only the sky
above Leverkusen is bright. Both of the old ones:
during the year of my birth;
in other cities; they looked after the farm.
The farm is the last one, and the boys build
apartments above the stalls. Flecks of rust,
dents; do we need the new canister?

ODERBRUCH

Die Kamera kaputt? Eine Kälte ist das, und
Krähen, größer als Krähen gewöhnlich sind, streichen
vereinzelt, flach drüben über die Felder.

Nichts drüben. Dämmerung. Gelb graue Dämmerung
breitet sich aus. Ein Baum in Polen ist
drüben der kahle verlorene Baum.

Leuchtend und leer fährt ein Bus übern Damm.
Am Ufer zwei Männer, mit dem Rücken
zum Damm, der weder anfängt noch aufhört.

Du hörst nichts. Du hörst das Geschiebe
der Schollen, der kreisenden Schollen. Du hörst
es lange noch, später, im Dunkel das treibende Eis.

Kaputt die Kamera, oder warum sind jetzt die Bilder
verwischt? Zwei Männer standen am Ufer. Sie
kamen zurück. Sie könnten erzählen.

ODERBRUCH

The camera's broken? It's cold out,
and there are crows bigger than crows
usually are, scattering smoothly over there across the fields.

Nothing over there. Twilight. Gold gray twilight
spreads out. A tree in Poland
is over there the lost barren tree.

Lighted and empty, the bus drives over the levee.
On the riverbank, two men with their backs
to the dam, which neither begins nor ends.

You don't hear anything. You hear the slippage
of the floe, the circling floe. You hear
for a long time yet, later, in the dark, the drifting ice.

The camera's broken, else why are the pictures
blurry now? Two men stood on the riverbank.
They came back. They could tell the story.

EINE VERBRAUCHTE MASCHIINE

Ölverluste, rostige Flanken; noch
fährt sie voll durch
jede Schicht. Das leise Keuchen
ist nur eine Gewohnheit, mit der sie
mitteilt: es gibt keinen Grund für
Beunruhigung. Problemfälle
übergeht sie mit ihrer Routine, und
überhaupt, alles Erfahrung. Gelernt
hat sie, daß eine Maschine nicht
klagt und keinen Anlaß zur Klage
gibt. Schwerer zurecht kommt sie
mit neuen Produkten; da wird es
ernst, was soll man machen. Schon
wieder tritt Öl aus, und neuerdings
gibt es ein ungewohntes Geräusch.
Die Maschine weiß, daß sie
gut ist, und sie weiß,
sie kann sich selber nicht helfen.

A WORN-OUT MACHINE

Oil leaks, rusty sides; yet
it drives on
through each effort. The quiet
wheezing is a habit through which it
communicates: there's no reason
for disturbance. It overcomes
difficulties with its routine,
and above all, experiences. It's learned
that a machine doesn't complain
and gives no cause for complaint.
It's harder to come to terms with new
products; that's when deciding what to do
gets serious. More oil drips
out, and what's more, now
there's an unaccustomed noise.
The machine knows it's good,
and it knows
it can't help itself.

Fast etwas Vergessenes

1

ein Sommergeräusch; mitten durch
grüne Weizenfelder ziehn holländische Züge,
und der Himmel ab Mittag ist weiß.
Gleichgültig ist wieder alles, ist nichts;
der Name des nächsten Ortes reicht bis
zum Horizont, bis zum Zaun, wohinter
der rote Traktor hervorkommt

2

und ich erwähnte die gläserne Sauberkeit,
die selbständigen Sprachbezirke,
die augenscheinlich größeren Duldsamkeiten
jener Stadt am Ontario-See,
wo jeder Morgen im Hotel
mit einem Blick aus dem Fenster began
auf landeinwärts fliegende Gänse,
aber eine Begegnung der falschen Vergleiche
ergab keinen weiteren Weg zwischen
getrennten Orten und Zeiten, und
die Wolken hüllten die Fluglinien ein

An Almost Forgotten Thing

1

a summer sound; through the middle
of green wheat fields, Dutch trains run,
and the sky is white in the afternoon.
Everything, nothing, is trivial again;
the name of the next place reaches
to the horizon, to the fence, behind which
the red tractor lurches forward

2

and I mentioned the glassy cleanness,
the independent language districts,
the seemingly larger tolerance
of that city on Ontario Lake
where each morning in the hotel
began with a glance out the window
onto the landward flying geese,
but a meeting of false comparisons
offered no further path
between places and times,
and the clouds shrouded the lines of flight

VORORT, SOMMER, NACHMITTAG

                 —so etwas von
einem silberen Himmel, ganz
ohne Ankündigung und plötzlich
wie das langsam aufsteigende Flugzeug, das
über dem Kirschbaum die Wolkendecke
erreicht—
        immer noch ist es schwül, und
der wach gewordene Mann im Liegestuhl
atmet schwer—

Suburb, Summer, Afternoon

                              — such a thing
from the silver sky, entirely
without warning, sudden
like the slow-climbing airplane
which reaches above the cherry tree
to the cloudbank —
                    still though, it's muggy
and the awakening man in the deck chair
breathes heavily —

WAS MAN KANN

Diesen Strich ziehe noch einmal, es sieht
ihn sonst keiner.

Mehr kann man nicht erwarten als
einige wenige Zeichen des Dabeigewesenseins.

Was tust du abends, wenn du dich
in ein alleinstehendes Haus zurückgezogen hast?

Eine Täuschung, die Verlängerung des Schweigens, denn
anfangen und aufhören kann man nicht.

WHAT WE CAN

Make this mark again, otherwise
no one will see it.

We can't expect more than
a few signs of having been around.

What do you do in the evenings
when you've returned to an isolated house?

An illusion, prolonging silence,
for to begin and to end — that we can't do.

AM MAUSPFAD; AUTOBAHNBAU

Der Zaun: steht geschrieben auf den Brettern
des Bauzauns um die Baustelle herum,
und vorbeigehend täglich glaube ich
weniger, daß es ein Zaun ist.

ON MOUSE'S WAY; ROAD CONSTRUCTION

The fence: it's written on the slats
of the construction fence all around the site,
and walking by every day, I believe
less and less that it's a fence.

SHAKESPEARE'S LAND

Landschaft zum Spielen; aber
wir spielen nicht; was ist,
fragen wir, mit der Belletristik.
Schafe auf den Hügeln, und Bagger
bewegen die Hügel; es ist
der Gemeinsame Markt. Später
die Ruhe des fließenden Mondes, und
wie der Luftkrieg anfing, denke ich,
Coventry nachts in der Nähe.

Shakespeare's Country

Landscape of play; but
we don't play; what's going on,
we ask, with belles lettres.
Sheep on the hills, and dredgers
move the hills; it's
an open market. Later
the flowing quiet of the moon,
how the air war began, I think,
and nearby, Coventry at night.

PARIS

Tage im grauen Marais
mit einem Schrecken zwischen den Schluchten
trennten wir uns abends und wortlos
half mir ein guter Dichter beim Warten
bis wir uns fanden und etwas tranken
an Tischen verwitterter Schönheit
zum Vergessen der Kälte
vor einem Weg zurück durch die Luft

PARIS

Days in gray Marais
with terror between the gorges
we parted ways wordlessly in the evening
a good poet helped me
until we found each other and drank
something at tables of weathered beauty
to forget the cold of the
path back through the air

A Foreign Affair

Die Schreibmaschine ging kaputt, ich sehe
Übersee-Flüge starten und höre das Schnarren
der ersten Rasenmäher; ein Nachkriegs-Film
und ich denke, wie ging,
wie geht es mir gut. In meiner Stille
passiert nichts? Anderswo
und ich schieße zurück. Nachmittags
in der Landschaft betrachtete ich die Folgen
dieses Frühlings; Gras wuchs schon
über die Flächen, die letztes Jahr brannten.

A Foreign Affair

The typewriter was broken — I see
international flights and hear the buzzing
of the first lawnmowers; a postwar film
I think, how well I was, am,
doing. In my quiet
nothing happens? Elsewhere,
and I shoot back. Afternoons
in the country — I considered the results
of this spring; grass was already growing
on the fields that were burning just last year.

DUBLIN IN BLOOMTIME

Diese wilden Gesichter
über dem still liegenden Fluß.
Nun verschwindet die Meute
mit dem geklauten Hut.
Dümpelnd zum Meer
bewegen sich grüne Flaschen hin.
Nachts mit gelb gewordenen Photos
kommt die Zeit mit Bloom.

DUBLIN IN BLOOMTIME

These wild faces
above the still river surface.
Then the pack of dogs disappears
with the stolen hat.
Green bottles sway seaward.
At night, with yellowing photos
time comes with Bloom.

BERICHT

Nichts war in deiner Abwesenheit.
Ich sah den Tulpen zu, den Blättern,
zwei oder drei, stündlich, fielen auf den Tisch.

Report

Nothing happened while you were away.
I watched the tulips, the petals;
two or three, hourly, fell on the table.

AUS DER GESCHICHTE DER GERÄUSCHE

Regenflächen Getreideflächen, dazwischen
der Tennisclub Glöbusch e.v. Nachts in den Büschen
rascheln die Flirts; am Tresen läßt einer
sich scheiden und macht mit dem Finger ticktack.

FROM THE HISTORY OF SOUNDS

Places of rain places of wheat, between them
the Glöbusch Tennis Club, LLC. At night, in the bushes,
the flirts rustle; at the bar, one is divorced
and taps a finger—*tap-tap-tap*.

NEBENAN

Du blickst aus dem Fenster,
Nachmittage, du rauchst, im Radio,
immer zu laut, Klavier-Programm,
trotzdem, manchmal höre ich, du singst.

Du sagst, ich bin nicht da,
wenn draußen das Telefon geht,
und ich glaube es dir wirklich,
nur kenne ich dein Versteck nicht.

Nearby

You look out the window.
Afternoons, you smoke,
while on the radio, always too loud,
a piano program, but still
sometimes, I hear you singing.

You say I'm not there
when the phone rings outside,
and I believe you, I do. It's only that
I don't know your hiding place.

DAS FENSTER AM ENDE DES KORRIDORS

Der Himmel, die Landschaft, der Fluß:
das Bild am Ende des Korridors.
Links und rechts die Appartements;
die Feuerlösch-Anlage. Das Summen des Aufzugs.
Die Zeit nach Büroschluß. Abweisende Gesichter,
kein Wort und keine Zärtlichkeit.

Jemand wird den Anfang machen
und an seiner Tür vorbeigehen
und weitergehen durch das Bild
hinaus in den Raum zum Fliegen.

THE WINDOW AT THE END OF THE CORRIDOR

The sky, the landscape, the river:
the painting at the end of the corridor.
The apartments to the left and right.
The fire extinguisher. The hum of the elevator.
The time after the offices close. Averted faces,
no word and no tenderness.
Someone will begin it,
and going by his door
and going farther, passed the painting,
out of the room, toward flight.

IN DER NÄHE VON ANDY WARHOL

als er dann wankte und umfiel,
der Schwarze auf den Union Square,
hob ich ans Auge die Kamera
und sah im Sucher, daß
er liegen blieb
zwischen den gehenden Leuten

Near Andy Warhol

as he then wobbled and fell over
the black man on Union Square,
I lifted the camera to my eye
and saw in the viewfinder
that he just lay there
between the people going by

SELBSTGESPRÄCH

Spree-Brücke, Kinder; Drachen
über der Spree, und
es dämmert; die Abendflüge
nach Westen; näher
der Herbst, so klirren
die Pappeln. Am Ufer,
ein Mann, im Selbstgespräch
hin und her, so
wird es nicht still.

SOLILOQUY

Spree-Brücke[2], children; kites
over the Spree, and
twilight falls; the evening flights
to the West; closer
to autumn, thus the poplars
rustle. By the shore,
a man, soliloquizing
back and forth — that's not how
peace is found.

---

2   Bridge in Berlin, over the river Spree.

DIE LAGE IM FEBRUAR

Nachmittags, zwischen vier und fünf, sieht es
schon anders aus. Die Vögel fallen
in die Gärten ein; die Luft nimmt langsam
die Farbe des Frosts an. Zu spät
für eine andere Stadt. Die Sonne läßt
auf den Hängen ein Licht zurück, das wie
amerikanische Kindheit ist, vierziger Jahre.
Der sich nähernde Mann beerdigt die Leute
und sammelt Geld für den Karnevalszug.

THE SITUATION IN FEBRUARY

Afternoons, between four and five, it looks
different. The birds collapse
upon the gardens; the air slowly takes
on the color of frost. Too late
for another city. The sun leaves
behind some light on the slopes,
which is like American childhood, in the Forties.
The approaching man buries people
and collects money for the carnival procession.

KÖLNER MÄRZ

Der Blick in den Hof; die Türkenkinder wissen
von der Bombennacht nichts. Im Mauerdurchbruch
steht der Container; Efeu wuchert
zwischen den Rissen hoch. Die Jungens trugen
Winteruniform; im Geäst gegenüber blieb
eine Mütze hängen, der Rest einer Gardine.

March in Cologne

The view of the courtyard; the Turkish children don't know
anything of the night bombings. In the breaking
of the Wall, a container stands; ivy grows high and wild
between the crevices. The youths wear
winter uniforms; in the branches across the way, a hat
hangs, and the remains of a curtain.

SEPTEMBERANFANG

Kein Krieg. Die alte Frau
zieht nur den Kopf ein, weil
sie hört, wir ein Apfel
krachend durchs Geäst schlägt.

Beginning of September

No war. The old woman
draws her head in, because
she hears an apple
crashing through the branches.

WAS DU SIEHST

Kurz drehen Scheinwerfer sich
durch die Kurve, und für Sekunden ist
das Zimmer hell. Dann siehst du
an der Wand den Schatten des Baums,
der kahl steht in diesem Sommer.

WHAT YOU SEE

The headlights turn briefly
through the curve, and for seconds
the room is bright. Then you see,
on the wall, the shadow of the tree
which stands barren this summer.

NACH DER BAUSTELLE

Ein wiedergefundenes Maisfeld; ohne zu suchen,
es lag plötzlich da, am Ende
der Pappelreihe, am Rand des Kanals.

Es war Anfang September,
und über den nassen Feldweg marschierte
die ungarische Armee.

Die Geschichte der Pappeln geht weiter;
geschrieben wird sie in Tagebüchern,
in kurzen Ferien, kurz vor der Offensive.

Der Mais reifte langsam; zuvor in den Jahren
Rüben, Roggen, Kartoffeln; zeitweise
Brachland, als der Kanal kam.

Past the Construction Site

A field of corn, found again; without looking,
it lay suddenly there, at the end
of the row of poplars, on the edge of the canal.

It was the beginning of September,
and over the wet country path
the Hungarian army marched.

The history of poplars continues;
it's written in diaries,
on short holidays, shortly before the offensive.

The corn grows slowly; in the years before—
beets, rye, potatoes; historically fallow
land, when the canal came.

IN MEMORIAM DONALD BARTHELME

Sommerregen. Schwarzer Abend. An den Rand
einer Todesmeldung gekritzelt die verfügbaren Daten,
die das Interview in Gang setzen, die Erinnerung
an entrückte Begegnungen, von denen
wir uns mehr Zukunft versprochen hatten.

Der neue *New Yorker* bleibt offen liegen.
Was heißt Zukunft, wenn sich das letzte Gespräch
per Bandschleife endlos wiederholen läßt und
ein Nachruf zehn Jahre liegt im Archiv.
Trockener Sommer. Der Abend ist hell.

Eine Reise ist vorzubereiten. Man muß
durch eine Nebelfront, deren Weiß so weiß
wie chinesische Trauer ist. Die Gerstenfelder sind leer,
und man liest, kompliziert sind die Städte.

In Memoriam Donald Barthelme

Summer rain. Black evening. On the edge
of a letter announcing a death, the available dates
are scribbled, setting an interview in motion,
the memory of nostalgic meetings, of which
we promised there'd be more in the future.

The current *New Yorker* lies open.
What does the future mean, when the last
talk loops endlessly and an obituary
lies for ten years in the archive.
Dry summer. The evening is bright.

There's a trip to prepare for. One must
go through a fog, the white of which so white
like Chinese grief is. The fields of barley
are empty, and one reads, the cities are complicated.

DIE HÖLLE, SAGTE SARTRE, DAS SIND DIE ANDEREN

L'heure bleu, könnte sein, aber es ist
der Heimwerker, der nach seinem und meinem Feierabend
die Stimmung macht. Machtlos dieses ganze Haus,
siebtes, elftes, vierzehntes Stockwerk; der Mann
bohrt in den Wänden, und man sieht
ihn nicht. Falls ich ihn sehe, werde ich,
werde ich nichts. Wie immer, Beschwerde geht
ins Gedicht, das Großen bleibenden Lärm macht.

HELL, SARTRE SAID, IS OTHER PEOPLE

L'heure bleu, it could be, but it's
the do-it-yourself handyman who makes the mood
for his and my evening. Powerless this entire building—
seventh, eleventh, fourteenth floor; the man
drills into the walls, yet no one
sees him. In case I see him, I'll, I'll
do nothing. Like always, complaints go
in the poem, which makes a large staying noise.

RENAISSANCE

Nun betrachte die Wiese, nicht
das Photo, die Wiese.

Die Katze, keine Bewegung,
und keine Bewegung, die Amsel.

Rostblätter unter dem Zaun.

Rostblätter unter dem Zaun.

Und Dämmerung, und wilder Schnee.

Der stille Schnee. In der Dämmerung
geht der Schnee.

Renaissance

Now observe the meadow, not
the photograph, the meadow.

The cat, no movement,
and no movement, the blackbird.

Rust-colored leaves below the fence.

Rust-colored leaves below the fence.

And twilight, and wild snow.

The quiet snow. In twilight,
the snow falls.

SAMSTAGMORGEN, KURZ VOR DEM FRÜHSTÜCK

Raschelnd kam die Dunkelheit,
Schnee war angesagt, der Kater
rettete noch einen Vogel, trug ihn
zwischen den Zähnen ins Haus.

Saturday Morning, Shortly before Breakfast

Darkness came rustling on;
snow was forecasted; the tomcat
saved one more bird, carried it
into the house, between his teeth.

GEGEN HALB FÜNF

nachmittags im Dezember kam plötzlich die Sonne
hinter der Wolkenwand hoch

eine Weile telefonierten wir
du hattest im Gang stehen müssen
im überfüllten Intercity bis nach Hannover
was war denn los

das Landschaftsbild gewinnt an Tiefe
wenn das Licht sich ausbreiten kann jetzt
immer noch in den leerstehenden Wäldern

wir sollten doch zusagen vielleicht sogar kommen
nun ja sagte ich die Stadt ist so entrückt
verstopft die Autobahn ab irgendwann
du weißt auch wenn du's nicht wahrhaben willst
gehört man nicht mehr dazu

die Einstellung regelt sich automatisch
so rasch die Rehe über die Straße wechseln
vor Wildunfällen wird gewarnt

gleichzeitig gegen halb fünf stand auch der Mond
überm Birnbaum unterwegs nach Nordosten

Around Four-Thirty

afternoon in December the sun suddenly came out
behind the cloudbank

we talked for a while on the phone
you had been forced to stand in the aisle
in the overfilled inter-city train as far as Hanover
what was wrong

the image of the landscape gains depth
when the light can beam out now
still yet in the forests that stand empty

we should then accept maybe even come
yeah well I said the city is so removed
the highway is clogged from sometime
you know it's true even if you don't want it to be
no one belongs there anymore

the blockage resolves itself automatically
so fast the deer cross the road
before accidents are warned of

at the same time, around four-thirty, the moon rose
above the pear tree, along the way toward the northeast

SAG MIR, WIE ES DIR GEHT

Oft müde. Die wirkliche Anstrengung besteht darin,
immer anwesend zu sein und Anwesenheit
zu beweisen. Je besser der Beweis gelingt, desto
ferner rückt der Horizont der Ruhe. Abends
schweigen die Erscheinungen, die Vorgänge nicht.
Bald ist es ein Privileg, die Fenster öffnen
zu können. Handlungen ohne Gefühle, und
das macht Vorteil. Eine zunehmende Starre
in den Augen. Hören worauf es ankommt.
Manchmal die Nähe von Wasser zu riechen
oder den grünen Himmel zu sehen, das sind jetzt
Wörter; Dinge und Erfahrungen nicht.

Tell Me How You're Doing

Often tired. The real effort comes from being
present always and proving presence. The better
the proof, the farther the horizon of calm recedes.
In the evening, appearances are silent, but not the events.
Soon it's a privilege to be able to open the window. Actions
without emotions, which is an advantage. An increasing
rigidity in the eyes. Listening to what's important.
Sometimes to smell the nearness of water, or to see
the green sky. But these are just words;
not things or experiences.

ZEIG MIR DIE SAISON

Mehr Kälte im neuen April, so preise
dieses kalifornische Rot; ich meine
die abgepackten Radieschen. Radio
wie im Sommer, bei offenen Fenstern,
wenn es so wäre, so war es, und
der Sturm schob ins Zimmer den Schnee.

Show Me the Season

More cold in new April, so precious
this Californian red; I mean
the packed away radishes. Radio
like in summertime, from open windows —
if only it were so; it was so,
and the storm pushed snow into the room.

DIE TAUSEND UND ERSTE STRASSE

Paul Nougé steht verdeckt von Georgette Magritte,
zwischen zwei Bäumen. Daneben,
Standbein und Spielbein, die Fäuste in den Hüften,
steht René Magritte.
Neben Paul Magritte steht Martha Nougé
mit dem Rücken zu mir und
blickt in den Wald. La Foret de Soignes.
Bruxelles, 1939.

THE THOUSAND AND FIRST STREET

Paul Nougé stands concealed by Georgette Magritte,
between two trees. Next to them,
support leg and kicking leg, fists on his hips,
stands René Magritte.
Beside Paul Magritte stands Martha Nougé
with her back to me
as she looks into the forest. La Foret de Soignes.
Bruxelles, 1939.

MÖGLICHKEITEN FÜR BILDER

Dunkler Baum vor einem hellen Haus.
Wunschkörper.
Die traurigen Augen beim Schließen der Türe.
Holz und Milch; eine Lampe.
Der Wind, der die Hand ausstreckt (im Zitat).
Bälle, aus dem Mund tropfend.
Frieden im Tal.
Geduld der Minen.
Nun wächst die Wiese durchs Haus.
Springend, über den Strich in der Luft.
Die Küsten des Exils (seit 1957).
Winteräste im Sommer.
Sieg des Wartens.
Fallende Birnen. Liegende Birnen.
Fahrrad am Horizont.
Soldaten und ein Fahrrad.
Nacht des 7. November.
Das Elend der Befreiten.
Glas, zwischen Figuren.
Menschengruppen vor dem Horizont.
Nebel; die Versteinerung des Nebels.

POSSIBILITIES FOR PAINTINGS

Dark Tree in front of a Bright House.
Wishbodies.
Sad Eyes at the Shutting of Doors.
Wood and Milk; a Lamp.
The Wind, which Extends the Hand (in quotes).
Balloons, Dripping from the Mouth.
Peace in the Valley.
The Patience of Landmines.
Now the Meadow Grows through the House.
Leaping, over a Mark in the Air.
The Coasts of Exile (since 1957).
Winter Branches in Summer.
Triumph of Waiting.
Falling Pears. Lying Pears.
Bicycle on the Horizon.
Soldiers and Bicycle.
The Night of the 7th of November.
The Misery of the Liberated.
Glass, between Figures.
Groups of People before the Horizon.
Fog; the Fossilization of Fog.

TIMING

Im Westen der Himmel wird schwarz.
Noch immer in den Himbeeren.
Beeil dich.

Laß dir Zeit.
Aber verschwinde nicht, zwischen den Sträuchern.
Im Westen der Himmel wird weiß.

Timing

In the west, the sky grows black.
Still yet in the raspberries.
Hurry up.

Take your time.
But don't disappear, between the bushes.
In the west, the sky grows white.

HOTEL BELGICA

Die Chefin löst Kreuzworträtsel.
Würde gern helfen, Blondine,
spreche kein Flämisch.
Gut der weiße Kabeljau.
Ihre Mädchen rauchen zuviel.
Ein Bier noch, noch eins.
Die Nacht wird sehr stürmisch,
wie die letzte; jetzt das Lexikon.
Kommt denn noch wer,
Matrose, Hotelgast, Gespenst.
Noch sind Sie schön; alternd
die Holzwände, Bänke und Spiegel.
Ausbeuterin, warum lächeln Sie nie?
Vorgestern auch schon mal hier,
ein Bier noch, am selben Tisch.
Hören Sie, ganz gewaltig, draußen,
die Brandung; oder was ist.
Buchstaben, Wörter; kein Flämisch
und lerne es nicht, ein Bier noch,
in dieser wortlosen Nacht.

HOTEL BELGICA

The concierge works her crossword puzzles.
I'd like to help, madam,
but no speak Flemish.
Her white codfish so good.
Her girls smoke too much.
Another beer, one more.
The night grows stormy,
like last night; and now the dictionary.
And who else is coming —
Sailor, hotel guest, a ghost.
You're still pretty; aging
the wooden walls, the seats and mirror.
Miss Exploiter, why don't you ever smile?
Day before yesterday and already here,
another beer, at the same table.
Listen — very violent, outside,
the breakers; or what is it.
Letters, words; no Flemish
and won't learn it; one more beer,
in this wordless night.

KORRESPONDENT

In die Kamera schaut er kaum; fast sieht es aus,
als führe er ein Selbstgespräch, eine Korrespondenz
mit Etwas auf dem unsichtbaren Tisch, vielleicht
mit dem Bleistift, der Zigarette.
Ein leichtes Zittern der Hände . . . man weiß nicht; jedenfalls
sehr sympatisch, nichts Gewisses, eher Genuschel, was
kann man schon sagen . . . Kälte und Blicke
auf eine Straße, die ein bißchen erhellt ist von
Schnee; eine übrig gebliebene Fahne, die
von einer Windmaschine bewegt wird. Riesiges, das langsam
verschwindet . . . es ist schon verschwunden, noch vor
einem Dekret. Er wiederholt es; er kann erst gehen, wenn
nichts mehr passiert. Man wird ihn vermissen.

CORRESPONDENT

He hardly looks into the camera; it almost seems
as though he were having a discussion with himself,
a correspondence
with Something on the invisible table, perhaps
with his pen or cigarette.
A light tremble of his hands . . . no one knows; in any case
very nice, nothing specific, just mumbling —
what can you say . . . coldness and glances
toward the street, which is somewhat lighted
with snow; a leftover flag
blown by a wind machine. Something gigantic that slowly
disappears . . . it has already disappeared, even before
any decree. He reiterates, he can only leave
once nothing else is happening. We'll miss him.

FRÜHE WARNUNG

eine Ebene die weiß war dann grün
jetzt ist es dunkel
und unentschieden die Jahreszeit
wie der Zwist der schweifenden Seelen
wenn sie unerlöst sind
raunte mein Pfarrer

Early Warning

a plain that was white then green
now it's dark
and undetermined the time of year
like the discord of wandering souls
when they are unsaved
whispers my pastor

OSTENDE

Die See prallt gegen die Fenster. Muscheln
mustern sich zwischen den Spielsälen ein;
würfelnd, alte Marineflieger.
Eine Fahne steigt auf und jener Kolonie
sind Perücken, Gewürze, Pensionen geblieben.
Die Skrupel zermürben die Sätze des Ruhms;
im Nachlaß wühlen Makler nach Münzen.

OSTENDE[3]

The sea surges against the windows. Mussels
examine themselves between the gambling rooms;
throwing dice, old marine pilots.
A flag is raised and of that colony
there are still wigs, spices, guest houses.
Scruples wear away at vainglorious words;
all over the estate, realtors burrow for coins.

---

3   Ostende is a small town on the Belgian coast, popular among Ger-
man tourists.

BILDBESCHREIBUNG

Das Bild einer Bucht, und die Bucht
ist gewesen, leer, und sanft,
an den Rändern. Der Name sagt
nichts mehr; es gibt keinen Namen,
und das Bild ist erfunden,
unbeschreibbar, wie all das hier herum.

Description of a Painting

The painting of a bay, and the bay
was, empty, and gentle,
along the shoreline. The name says
nothing more; there isn't a name,
and the painting is a fiction,
indescribable, like everything around here.

EINE DER VIELEN GERÄUSCH-ERZÄHLUNGEN

Es war ein ruhiger Nachmittag.
Draußen, auf dem Korridor, hörte ich
eine Türe zuschlagen
und das Weinen einer Frau, das sich
langsam entfernte. Dann hörte ich die Türe
noch einmal, aber es blieb still.

One of the Many Stories of Sounds

It was a quiet afternoon.
Outside, in the corridor, I heard
a door slam
and a woman's crying, which
slowly diminished in the distance.
Then I heard the door
again, though it stayed silent.

DRAUSSEN, STADTGRENZE

Die fallenden Blätter; es ist das Geräusch
am Tage Allerheiligen. Letzte Bewegung
des Sommers, mit dem Geruch
der Chrysanthemen. Wir müssen, komm,
über die Friedhöfe gehen; die Erde
ist feucht, vorüber der Krieg.

Outside, City Limit

The falling leaves; it is the sound
on All Saint's Day. Last movement
of summer, with the scent
of chrysanthemums. We must go, come now,
across the cemeteries; the earth
is moist, and the war over.

FRÜHER ODER SPÄTER

Rosen, Getreide, Holunder; in diesem Juni
alles weit weg, da unten. Gefühle
mehr und mehr auf Distanz; wir werden
auf diesem Meer nicht weit kommen.
Auf unseren Bildern sehen wir, wie
es war, aber nicht, was dann kam.

SOONER OR LATER

Roses, wheat, elderberries; this June
everything far away, down below. Sensations
more and more distanced; we won't come
very far on this sea.
We look at our pictures, how
it was, but not what came after.

ZEHNTER JULI

Ginster; mit einer Ansichtskarte
von der Insel Elba kommt Ginster ins
Haus; Proust hat Geburtstag; und
es kommt die Erinnerung an Ginster
in den Jahren, als am Bahndamm
nicht blühte der Ginster.

TENTH OF JULY

Gorse; with a postcard
from Elba island gorse comes
into the house; it's Proust's birthday;
and the memory of gorse
in those years when, along the railway,
the gorse didn't bloom.

DORFRAND MIT TANKSTELLE / 1

Jetzt ist Juli, und es ist heiß
wie im Juli, sagt Moritz der Tankwart.
Im Winter macht die Waschanlage nur Verlust.
Staubfahnen ziehen hinter dem Landrover her,
der den Feldweg verläßt. Wenn der Bauantrag
durchkommt . . . der Eigentümer wiegelt ab.
Natur bliebt Natur. Moritz sagt, früher
war der Tankwart der Tankwart. Dropsrollen,
Kaugummi und Gummibärchen, morgens
die Remittenden . . . man kann es,
sagt Moritz, nicht sehen, aber das Benzin
ist da. Im Winter die Winterreifen, sonst
zahlt die Versicherung nichts. Der Landrover
rollt in die Waschanlage und zieht
die Antenne ein. Hinterher kann alles
zu spät sein, sagt Moritz, und früher
gab es eine Tränke hier für die Pferde.

VILLAGE OUTSKIRTS WITH GAS STATION / 1

Now it's July, and it's hot
like it is in July, says Moritz the station attendant.
In winter, the carwash just loses money.
Dust flags trail behind the Land Rover
leaving the dirt road. When the building application
comes through . . . that appeases owners.
Nature is still nature. Moritz says, earlier
the station attendant was the station attendant. Fruit rolls,
chewing gum, and Gummy Bears, mornings
the returns . . . you can't,
says Moritz, see it, but the gasoline
is there. In winter, the snow tires, otherwise
the insurance won't pay out. The Land Rover
rolls into the carwash and retracts
the antenna. Afterwards everything can be
too late, says Moritz, and earlier
there was a trough for the horses.

DORFRAND MIT TANKSTELLE / 2

Gestern. Der Benzinpreis. Alles war gestern,
sagt Moritz der Tankwart, Krieg und Antikrieg.
Er schaut auf die Straße und hebt den Arm, als
der Traktor vorbeikommt und der Fahrer
den Arm hebt. Wir leben vom Öl, oder
wir sterben. Der Mais hat noch Zeit.

Aber der Roggen steht kurz. Zu kurz
steht der Roggen. Der Traktorfahrer hält und holt
sich ein paar Pflaumen vom Baum. Die Wiese
läßt er liegen. Die Wiese liegt verdorrt.

Brüssel warnt. Die Eifel fängt den Seewind ab.
Der Osten baut keine Wolken mehr, und drüben
stehen alte Leute am Zaun. Der Schatten des Giebels
wandert, bis er stürzt in die offene Scheune.

Morgen ist Dienstag. Bis dahin bleiben die Ziffern
stabil. Moritz legt den Hörer auf und sieht
den Pickup in die Einfahrt biegen. Die Möhrensäcke
für den Reiterhof. Der Tankwart weiß Bescheid:
Früher Kavallerie. Alles war früher, das Morgenrot
auf den Wiesen, Patrouillen unter den Pflaumen.

VILLAGE OUTSKIRTS WITH GAS STATION / 2

Yesterday. The price of gasoline. Yesterday everything was,
says Moritz the gas station attendant, war and anti-war.
He looks down the road and raises his arm, as
the tractor goes by and the driver
raises his arm. We're living on oil, or
we're dying. The corn still has time.

But the rye is short. Too short
is the rye. The tractor driver stops and picks
himself a few plums from the tree. He lets
the field just lie there. The field lies there all dried up.

Brussels warns. The Eifel Mountains intercept the sea's breeze.
The East no longer builds clouds, over there
the elderly stand at the fence. The shadow of the gable
wanders until it plunges into the open barn.

Tomorrow is Tuesday. Until then the numbers
will stay stabile. Moritz hangs up the phone and sees
the pickup bending in the entrance. The bags of carrots
for the horse ranch. The station attendant knows for certain:
Earlier, cavalry. Everything was earlier, the sunrise
over the fields, patrols beneath the plums.

NEUE SACHLICHKEIT

Da hat es gestanden, das Eckhaus
zwischen den Straßen nach Werne und Witten.
Stern Pils. Persil.
Die Straßen hat der Maler leer
gemalt, Winter 69.
Noch ein Name steht, vielleicht der Name
des Wirts, unlesbar über der Tür.
Der Maler Günter Senge lebt
nicht mehr, und man sieht keine Maler
am Ufer der Emscher.
Es gibt das Grau
des Himmels, der Häuser. Es gibt
vier Bäume, zwei Masten, eine Reihe Geländer.

New Objectivity

It stood there, the house on the corner
between the streets to Werne and Witten.
Stern Pilsner. Persil.
The streets were empty
in the painter's painting, Winter 69.
One last name is there, perhaps the name
of the landlord, illegible above the door.
The painter Günter Senge lives
no longer, and no one sees painters
along the waterfront of the Emscher.
There is the gray
of the sky, of houses. There are
four trees, two masts, one row of handrails.

WETTERBERICHT

Keine Leute gesehen. Zuhause
mache ich das Radio an . . . es warnt,
Unwetter, Blitzeis, etc. Draußen
war es so angenehm, milde, still
und leer in den Straßen.

WEATHER REPORT

No people seen. At home,
I turn the radio on . . . it warns
of stormy weather, black ice, etc. Outside
it was so comfortable, mild, calm
and empty in the streets.

ALTER FILM

Der Geruch, der im Haus hängt,
verbrannte Kartoffeln. Als wir auf den Feldern
an den Feuern hockten, hatten wir
den großen Bruder, West oder Ost, der Wind
war immer stark. In dieser Kindheit,
nach jedem Brand, blieben auch
die Sterne klar, und als
die Front vorbei war, raubten wir, es waren
die Wälder der Feinde, unser Holz.

OLD FILM

The scent hanging in the house,
burnt potatoes. As we hunkered around the fires
in the fields, we had big brother, West or East;
the wind was always strong. In this childhood,
after every blaze,
the stars remained clear, and when
the front was past, we robbed
the foes' forests, our wood.

Jahrgang 1932

Dies sind Fotografien der Küste, so sahen
Bunker aus. Frag deinen alten Vater, den Architekten,
was der Atlantikwall war —
                    »Pendant ma jeunesse,
le littoral européen était interdit au public
pour cause de travaux; on y bâtissait un mur
et je ne découvris l'Océan
qu'au cours de l'été 45«: Paul Virilio,
Jahrgang 1932 —
                    liegend am Strand, radelnd
in den Dünen; Wehrbezirk Niederlande,
15. Festungspionierstab. Die Arbeit
von Wind und Sand am Vergessen; wie ein Kopf
ragt dieser Kommandoturm —
                    viel Zeit
für Archäologie, und eine Ausstellung im Museum
der dekorativen Künste, Paris; Zitate im Katalog
von Hölderin, Rilke, Ernst Jünger.
                    Eingegraben
im Sand, mein Kopf der Bewußtseinsturm;
grabt ihn aus,
            Spuren zum *Zeitgeist*; später
Entzücken, Entsetzen —
                    dies sind Fotos:
See und Sand kommen zurück. Kinder, neu
und blond, rennen und bauen im Schlamm.

THE YEAR 1932

These are photographs of the coast; this is how
bunkers looked. Ask your old man, the architect,
what the Atlantic Wall was—
                         "Pendant ma jeunesse,
le littoral européen était interdit au public
pour cause de travaux; on y bâtissait un mur
et je ne découvris l'Océan
qu'au cours de l'été 45": Paul Virilio,
the year 1932—
                         lying on the beach, bicycling
among the dunes; Netherlands Military District
15. Defense reconnaissance team. The work
of wind and sand on forgetfulness; like a head
this command tower looms—
                         plenty of time
for archeology, and an exhibit in the museum
of decorative arts, Paris; in the catalog, quotes
from Hölderin, Rilke, Ernst Jünger.
                         Buried
in the sand, my head, a tower of consciousness;
dig it out,
         tracks leading to the *Zeitgeist*; later
delight, horror—
                 these are photos:
sea and sand return. Children, new
and blond, run and build in the muck.

APPENDIX

Dorfrand mit Tankstelle **(2007)**
"Dorfrand mit Tankstelle / 1"; "Dorfrand mit Tankstelle /
2"; "Kölner März"; "Septemberanfang"; "Gegen halb fünf";
"Neue Sachlichkeit"; "Die Lage im Februar"; "Wetterbericht"

Foxtrott im Erfurter Stadion **(1993)**
"Oderbruch"; "Eine vorläufige Topographie"; "Eine
verbrauchte Maschine"; "Herbstgeschichte"; "Was man kann";
"Im Wind"; "Zwei Frauen"; "Korrespondent"; "Sonne oder
Mond"; "Chronik"; "Vorort, Sommer, Nachmittag" ; "Fast
etwas Vergessenes"; "Timing"; "Nochmals"; "Sonntagabend"

In der verbleibenden Zeit **(1979)**
"Frühe Warnung"; "Alter Film"

Erzähl mir nichts vom Krieg **(1977)**
"Sag es mir, wie es dir geht"; "Das Fenster am Ende
des Korridors"; "Vier Zeilen"; "Früher oder später";
"Möglichkeiten für Bilder"; "Wetterbericht"; "Eine der vielen
Geräusch-Erzählungen"; "Die Hölle, sagte Sartre, das sind die
Anderen"; "A Foreign Affair"; "Die tausend und erste Straße";
"Draußen, Stadtgrenze"; "Zeig mir die Saison"

Das Ende der Landschaftsmalerei **(1974)**
"Vormittag; Zusammenhang"; "Bezirk Tiergarten";
"Shakespeare's Land"; "Gedicht mit Fragen"; "Einst, im
Februar"; "Am Mauspfad; Autobahnbau"; "Zehnter Juli";
"In der Nähe von Andy Warhol"; "Bildbeschreibung";
"Selbstgespräch"

Schnee **(1971)**
"Gedicht über Schnee im April"; "Gedicht aus Köln"

ABOUT THE AUTHOR

JÜRGEN BECKER was born in Cologne, Germany, in 1932. He is the author of more than thirty books of drama, fiction, and poetry—all published by Suhrkamp, Germany's premier publisher. He has won numerous prizes, including the Heinrich Böll Prize, the Uwe Johnson Prize, the Hermann Lenz Prize, and the Georg Büchner Prize, the highest honor a German-language author can receive.

ABOUT THE TRANSLATOR

OKLA ELLIOTT is an assistant professor at Misericordia University. He holds a PhD in comparative literature from the University of Illinois and an MFA in creative writing from Ohio State University. His nonfiction, poetry, short fiction, and translations have appeared in *Cincinnati Review*, *Harvard Review*, *Indiana Review*, *The Literary Review*, *New York Quarterly*, *Prairie Schooner*, *A Public Space*, and *Subtropics*, among others. His books include *From the Crooked Timber* (short fiction), *The Cartographer's Ink* (poetry), and *The Doors You Mark Are Your Own* (a coauthored novel).